Earth's Moon

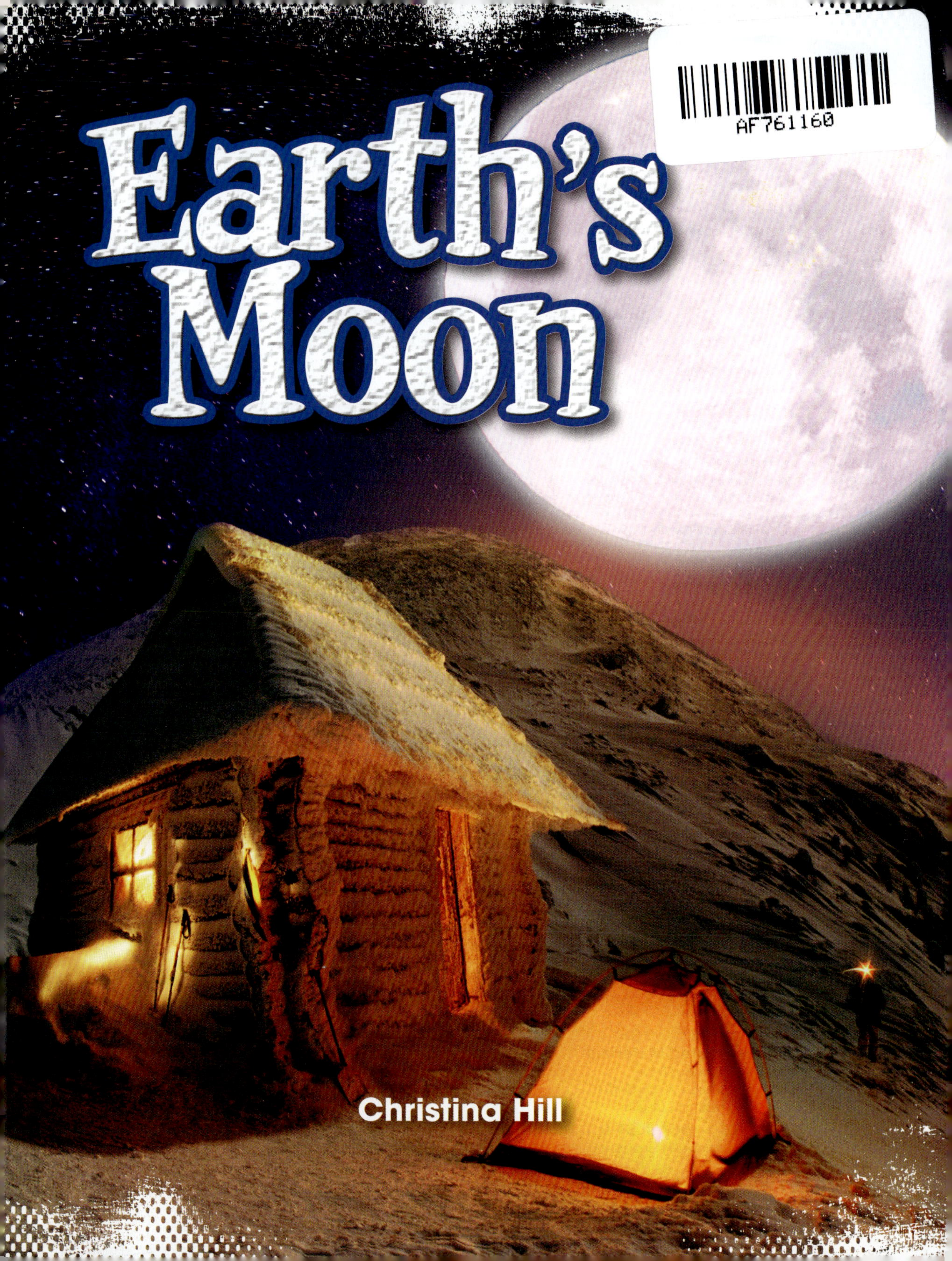

Christina Hill

Consultant

Sean Goebel, M.S.
University of Hawaii
Institute for Astronomy

Image Credits: p.8 (top left) Dea G. Dagli Orti/ age fotostock; p.5 (bottom) Paul Brown/Alamy; p.4 (top) Stocktrek Images, Inc./Alamy; p.7 (top) Robin Canup/Encyclopedia Britannica; pp.10–11 (top & bottom), 12 (top), 13 (top) 14 (top) (illustrations) Tim Bradley; pp.26–27 (illustrations) Lexa Hoang; pp.28–29 (illustrations) J.J. Rudisill; pp.2–5 (background), 6–7, 10–11 (background), 13 (background & bottom), 14–15 (background), 15 (bottom right, 16 (bottom), 18–19 (background), 21 (top), 22 (left) 22–23 (background), 24–25 (background), 25 (top), 26–27 (background), 21 (background), 24 (left), 30–31 iStock; pp.8–9 (background) David A. Hardy/ Science Source; p.18 (left) Detlev van Ravenswaay/ Science Source; p.23 (top right) GIPhotoStock/ Science Source; pp.16–17 (background) SPL/Science Source; p.19 (top) Wellcome Images/Science Source; p.20 (left) Wikimedia Commons; all other images from Shutterstock.

Library of Congress Cataloging-in-Publication Data

Hill, Christina, author.
Earth's moon / Christina Hill.
pages cm
Summary: "Our moon is magnificent. Sometimes, it appears in the night sky as a massive glowing disk. Other nights, it can't be seen at all. Without the moon, our world would be a different place"—Provided by publisher.
Audience: K to grade 3
Includes index.
ISBN 978-1-4807-4651-0 (pbk.)
ISBN 1-4807-4651-7 (pbk.)
ISBN 978-1-4807-5095-1 (ebook)
1. Moon—Juvenile literature.
2. Moon—Phases—Juvenile literature.
3. Earth (Planet)—Juvenile literature. I. Title.
QB582.H55 2015
523.3--dc23
2014034282

Teacher Created Materials
5301 Oceanus Drive
Huntington Beach, CA 92649-1030
http://www.tcmpub.com

ISBN 978-1-4807-4651-0

Table of Contents

Mysteries of the Moon

Walking at night under a bright white moon is a wonderful feeling. The moon has been worshipped for thousands of years for this reason. People have admired its power over the tides, plants, and animals. It has inspired spells, songs, and stories. And we have long wondered about its many mysteries.

Have you ever wondered why the moon seems to change? Sometimes, it's a full moon. It looks like a big circle. Other times, it's a tiny sliver, or **crescent**. And sometimes, the moon may not be seen at all.

A Closer Look

Astronomers studied the moon closely in the 17th century. An Italian scientist named Galileo was one of the first people to use a telescope to sketch the moon. It allowed him to see the surface of the moon more clearly.

With the moon, things are often not what they seem. It may look as though the moon is changing shape. But the moon isn't really changing. It's **orbiting** around Earth. It's a simple movement. But the motions of the moon have big effects. And today, scientists are still unraveling its many mysteries.

Lantern Festival

Yi Peng is a festival in Thailand in which thousands of paper lanterns are released into the night sky for good luck. The festival takes place during the full moon in November.

Phases of the Moon

Earth and the moon are always moving. Earth **revolves** around the sun. And the moon revolves around Earth. Earth also spins like a top! Each day, Earth makes one full rotation.

The moon orbits around Earth about once a month. Every year, Earth and the moon make their revolution around the sun.

Spinning in Circles

Earth rotates on its axis, while at the same time, revolves around the sun.

A Whacky Idea

Where did the moon come from? Scientists call what happened the *Big Whack*. They think Earth collided with a smaller object about 4.5 billion years ago. When the two objects hit, they sent large rocks flying into space. Over time, these rocks came together to form the moon. (The colors in the picture above show how the objects grew hotter after the collision.)

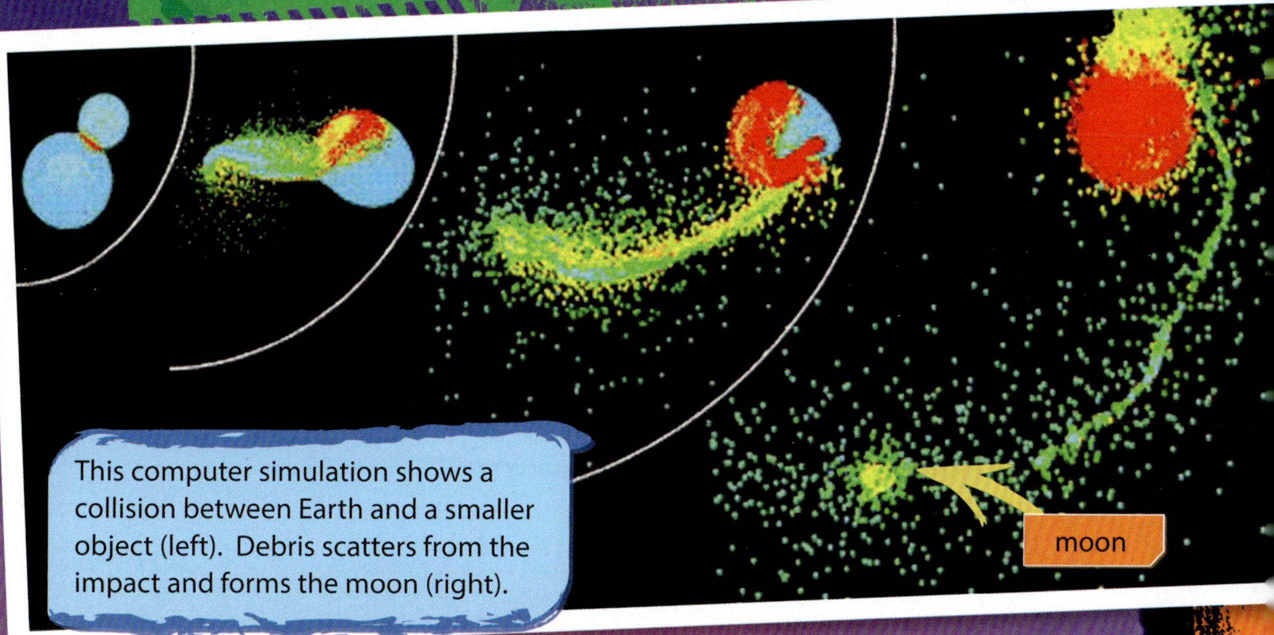

This computer simulation shows a collision between Earth and a smaller object (left). Debris scatters from the impact and forms the moon (right).

The moon may appear bright in the night sky. It may look as though it is producing a lot of light. But unlike the sun, the moon does not produce any light. Instead, it reflects the light from the sun. The moonlight we see is really reflected sunlight.

Tracking Time

Ancient people calculated that it takes 29.53 days from one new moon phase to the next. This is called a **lunar** month. They used the lunar month to construct a lunar calendar. This helped them keep track of time.

Long ago, people didn't have calendars or clocks like we do today. Instead, they **observed** the changes of the moon at night. They used the moon to record time.

Each day of the month, the moon moves. Sunlight hits a different part of the moon as it rotates. The moon doesn't change shape. But it looks different to us on Earth. This is because we can only see the part that is lit by the sun. The other part of the moon is in the sun's shadow. It appears dark to us.

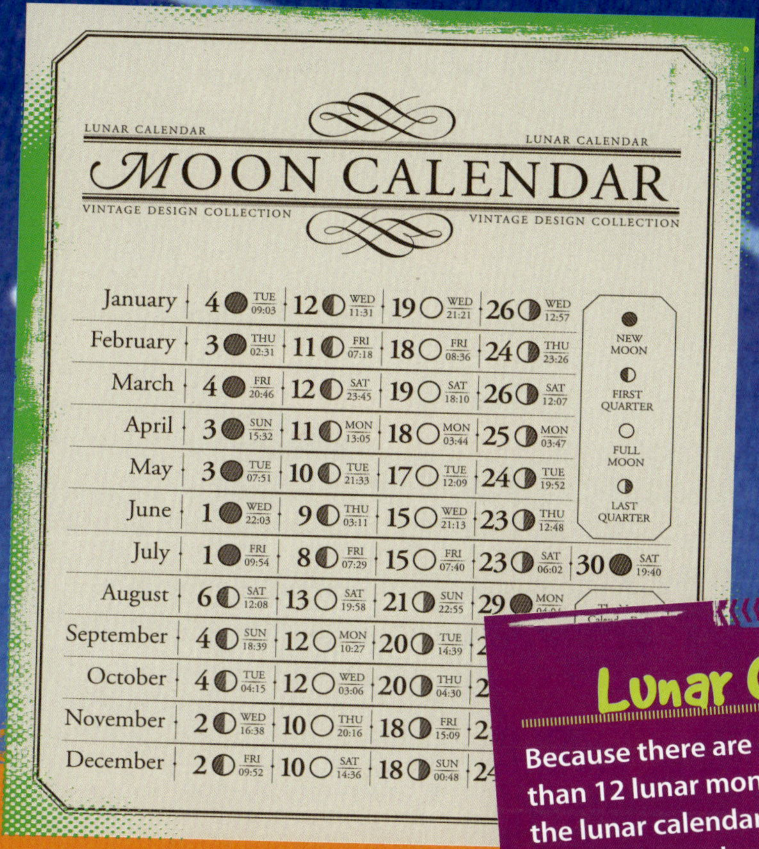

Lunar Calendar

Because there are slightly more than 12 lunar months in a lunar year, the lunar calendar doesn't quite match our modern calendar. But the Islamic calendar still uses the lunar system to mark religious holidays.

People long ago noticed that the moon follows the same pattern every four weeks. They also learned that there are eight phases of the moon. A phase occurs each time the moon appears to change shape.

The first phase of the moon is called the *new moon*. This is when the moon is between Earth and the sun. The side of the moon that faces us is in the shadow. We can't see it at all. During this phase, the moon is closer to the sun in the sky, and they rise and set at similar times.

The moon orbits Earth. After a few days, a tiny sliver of the moon begins to appear. This phase is called **waxing** crescent. The moon is said to be waxing when it appears to grow in the sky. But the moon isn't actually growing in size. Bit by bit, more of it is lit up each night.

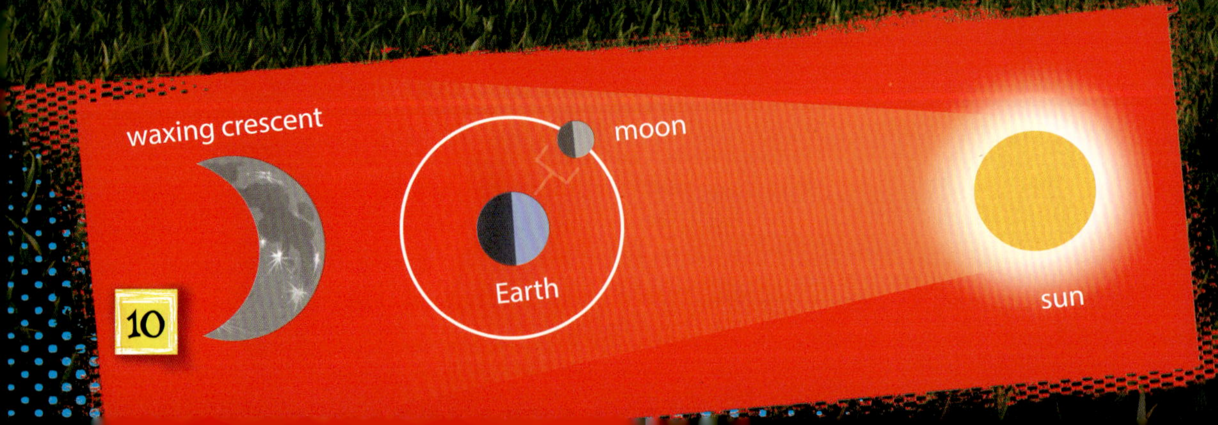

The Far Side of the Moon

The moon rotates at about the same rate that it revolves around Earth. That means the same side of the moon is always facing the planet. The far side of the moon has only been photographed by spacecraft. Grab a friend to see how this works.

1. Pretend you are Earth. Spin in place very slowly to represent a day passing.
2. Have your friend pretend to be the moon. The moon should spin as it revolves around you.
3. Try going at different speeds until you both find a speed at which each time you see the moon, you see your friend's face. This is how the moon orbits Earth.
4. Now, find another friend to play the sun. As Earth, you'll revolve slowly around the sun. And the moon will continue to revolve around you. Look to see who is moving the fastest and who is moving the slowest.

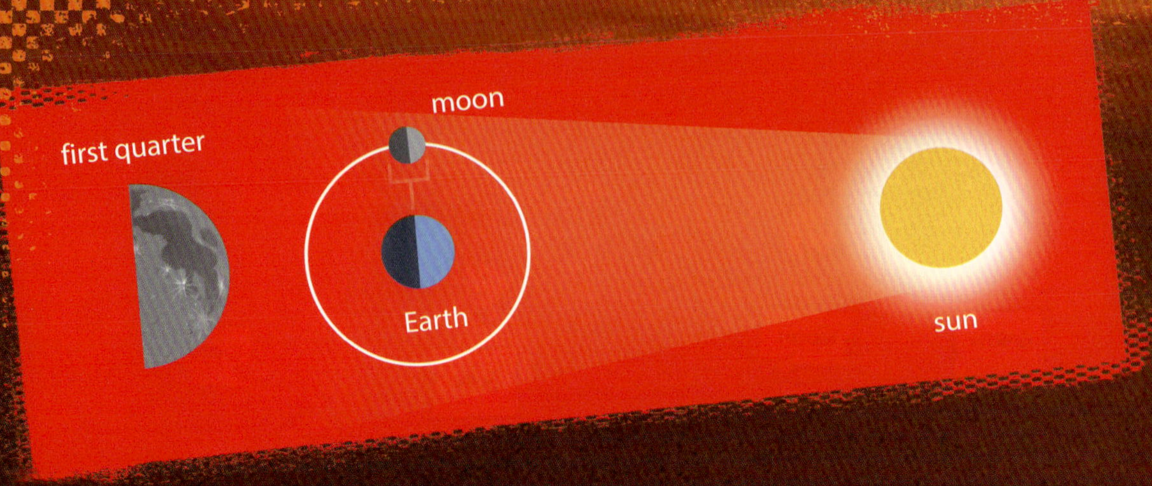

As the moon travels around Earth, the part that we can see increases to a larger crescent shape. Soon we will see one half of the moon. This happens when the moon has finished a quarter of its revolution around Earth. So, this phase is called the *first quarter*. The moon will be visible for the first half of the night. Then, the moon will set early before the sun rises. This leaves the sky dark in the early morning hours.

The next phase is called the *waxing gibbous* (GIB-uhs). During this phase, the moon appears almost completely full. The moon can be seen in the sky through most of the night.

Lined Up

A solar eclipse occurs when the moon passes between Earth and the sun, blocking all or a portion of the sun. A lunar eclipse occurs when Earth passes between the moon and the sun and Earth's shadow hides the moon or a portion of it.

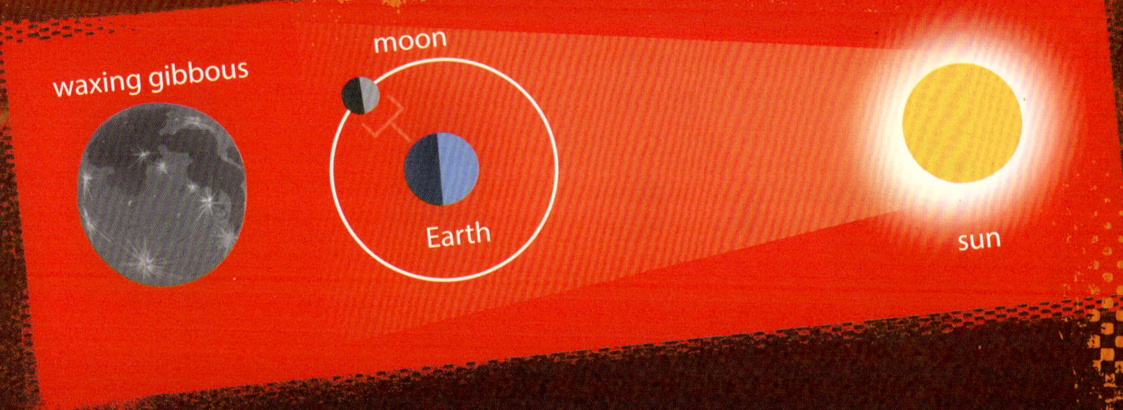

waxing gibbous moon

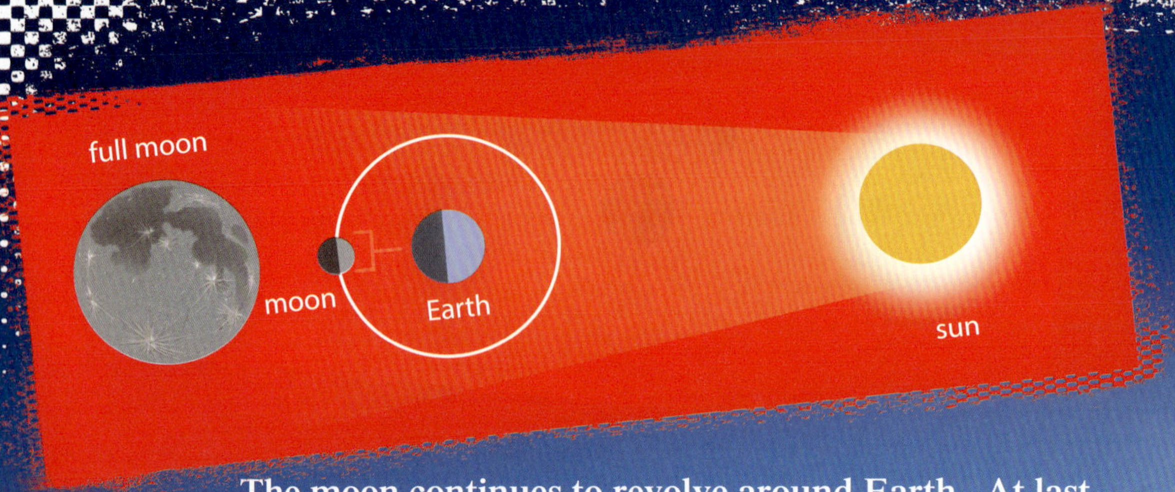

The moon continues to revolve around Earth. At last, we can see the full moon! During this phase, the moon will rise in the sky in the east. The sun sets in the west. The giant circle will shine brightly through the night. The full moon phase marks the halfway point in the moon's journey around Earth. Then, the phases start over again. But now, they occur in reverse order. The moon must make its way to the other side of its orbit. The moon will go through three more stages. It will appear to get smaller and smaller. At this time, the moon is said to be **waning**.

The moon may look round from Earth, but it's shaped slightly like an egg. The larger end faces Earth.

Once in a Blue Moon

Have you ever heard the phrase *once in a blue moon*? It means something happens very rarely. A blue moon is the second full moon in one month. It can also be the third full moon in a season with four moons. That doesn't happen very often!

During the *waning gibbous*, the moon looks like a full moon minus a tiny sliver. Next is the last quarter moon. Here we can see half of the moon lit up. The eighth phase is called *waning crescent*. During this phase, we can only see a tiny sliver of the moon. Then, the moon will return to the new moon phase. The moon has completed one full revolution around Earth. We will be able to see the moon again a few days later as it enters the waxing crescent phase again.

waning gibbous moon

Saturn and its moons

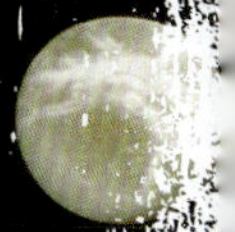

Many Moons

Earth isn't the only planet with a moon. Mars has two moons. And Saturn has many moons! Scientists have spotted 53 so far.

The Surface

The moon is a very different place from Earth. There is no liquid water on the surface of the moon. That means there are no oceans, rivers, or lakes. The surface of the moon is made of rock and soft dust.

The moon's surface is covered in big, deep holes called **craters**. Huge rocks, called *meteorites*, crash into the moon and leave behind craters. When they crash, these meteorites cause an explosion. The blast pushes rocks away from the center of the crater.

The moon also has volcanoes. They erupted a very long time ago. But we can still see the big pools of hardened lava they left behind on the surface of the moon.

Moon Rocks

Many craters are full of basalt. Basalt is a heavy gray rock. Nearly 20 percent of the near side of the moon is basalt.

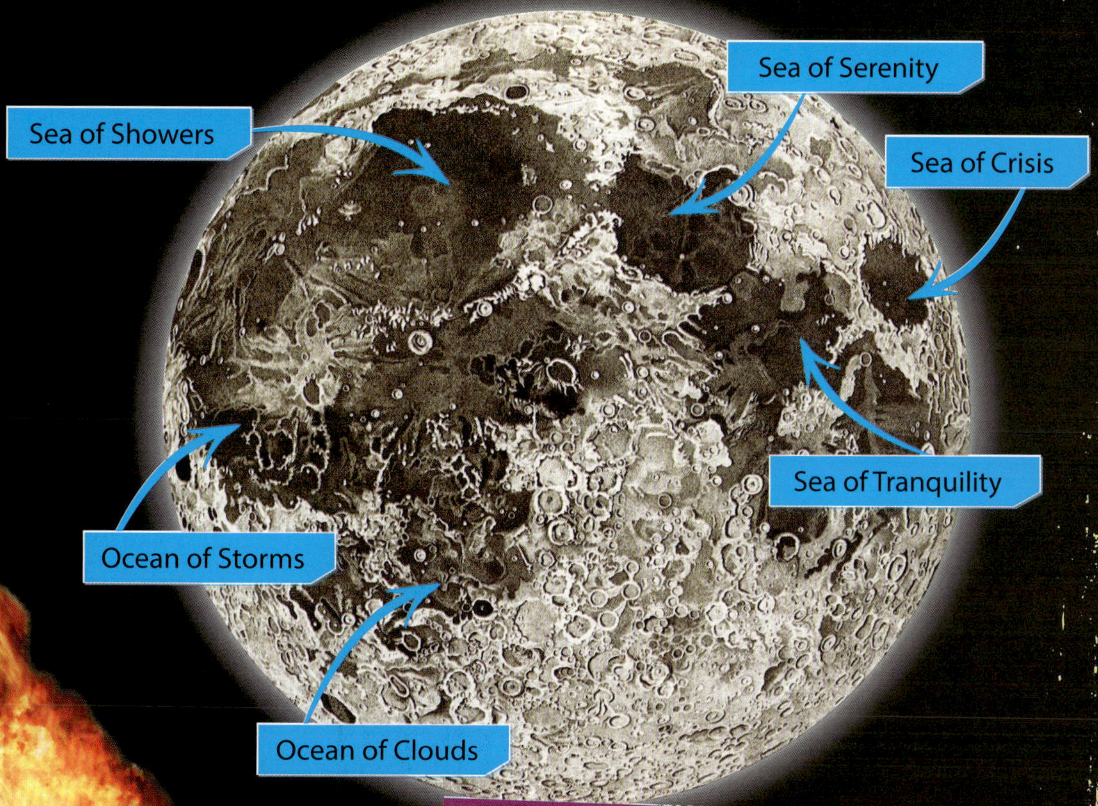

Lunar Lakes

When Galileo first looked at the moon through a telescope, he thought the dark areas he saw were water. He called them *seas*. The name stuck even after later scientists proved that the dark areas were formed when lava once flowed on the moon.

Atmosphere

There is no wind or rain on the moon. Unlike Earth, the moon has no weather. This is because there is very little air surrounding the moon. The air around Earth keeps temperatures from getting too hot or too cold. It also creates weather. Since the moon doesn't have this layer of air, it can get very hot during the day. It also gets very cold at night.

Sometimes, the moon may appear to change color. But this has more to do with Earth's air than the moon itself. When the air in Earth's sky bends the light, it can make the moon appear red, orange, brown, or gray. When the moon looks deep red, it is said to be a *blood moon*.

Without weather, any mark on the moon's surface will stay there for a long time. This is why there are so many craters on the moon. If nothing disturbs them, footprints made by astronauts on the moon might still be there in 10 million years!

Scientists use robots and advanced computers to study the moon.

blood moon

Extreme Temperatures

It can get as cold as -240° Celsius (-400° Fahrenheit) on the moon. During the day, the temperature can reach 120°C (250°F)!

Tides

Have you ever been to the ocean? Sometimes, the water level is high on the shore. This is called *high tide*. At low tide, the water goes down. More of the shore is visible. The moon causes this motion.

The moon and Earth are like magnets. The moon pulls Earth toward it. And the water in Earth's oceans is pulled, too. This pull creates a bulge in the water on both sides of the planet. As the moon and Earth rotate, it creates two high tides and two low tides each day.

Tides

When the tides are very high or very low, they are called *spring tides*. The opposite of spring tides are neap tides. Neap tides only create a small difference in water level. Both of these occur twice a month.

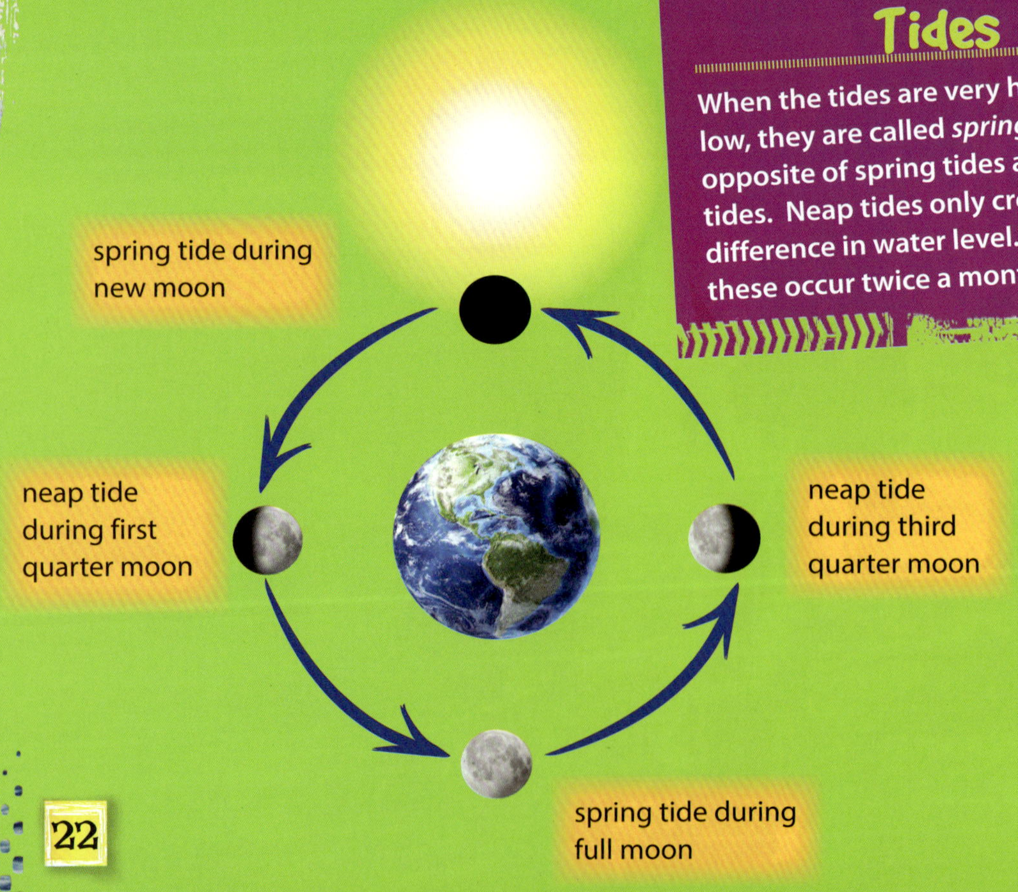

high tide

low tide

The highest tide height difference is in the Bay of Fundy in Canada: 15 meters (50 feet)!

Man on the Moon

People have always had questions about the moon. And many have dreamed of visiting it. It took thousands of years. But finally, in 1969, NASA astronauts Neil Armstrong and Buzz Aldrin landed on the moon. They were the first people to visit this strange new world. They gathered samples of rocks. They put up a U.S. flag. They also hung a sign to show they had been there.

The moon has less **gravity** than Earth. So the astronauts had lots of fun jumping there. Gravity is a force that pulls you to the ground. It keeps you from floating away. Because there was little gravity, the astronauts weighed less on the moon. This helped them bounce high!

Left Behind

The first trip to the moon was dangerous. Scientists weren't sure they could get the astronauts home. To make the trip easier, they wanted them to pack lightly. So on the way home, the astronauts left behind bags of urine! The moon is also now home to hammers, boots, and lots of other space trash.

Discovering Gravity

Isaac Newton studied the moon's movement to better understand gravity. He was the first to explain why the moon stays in orbit around Earth, rather than flying off into space.

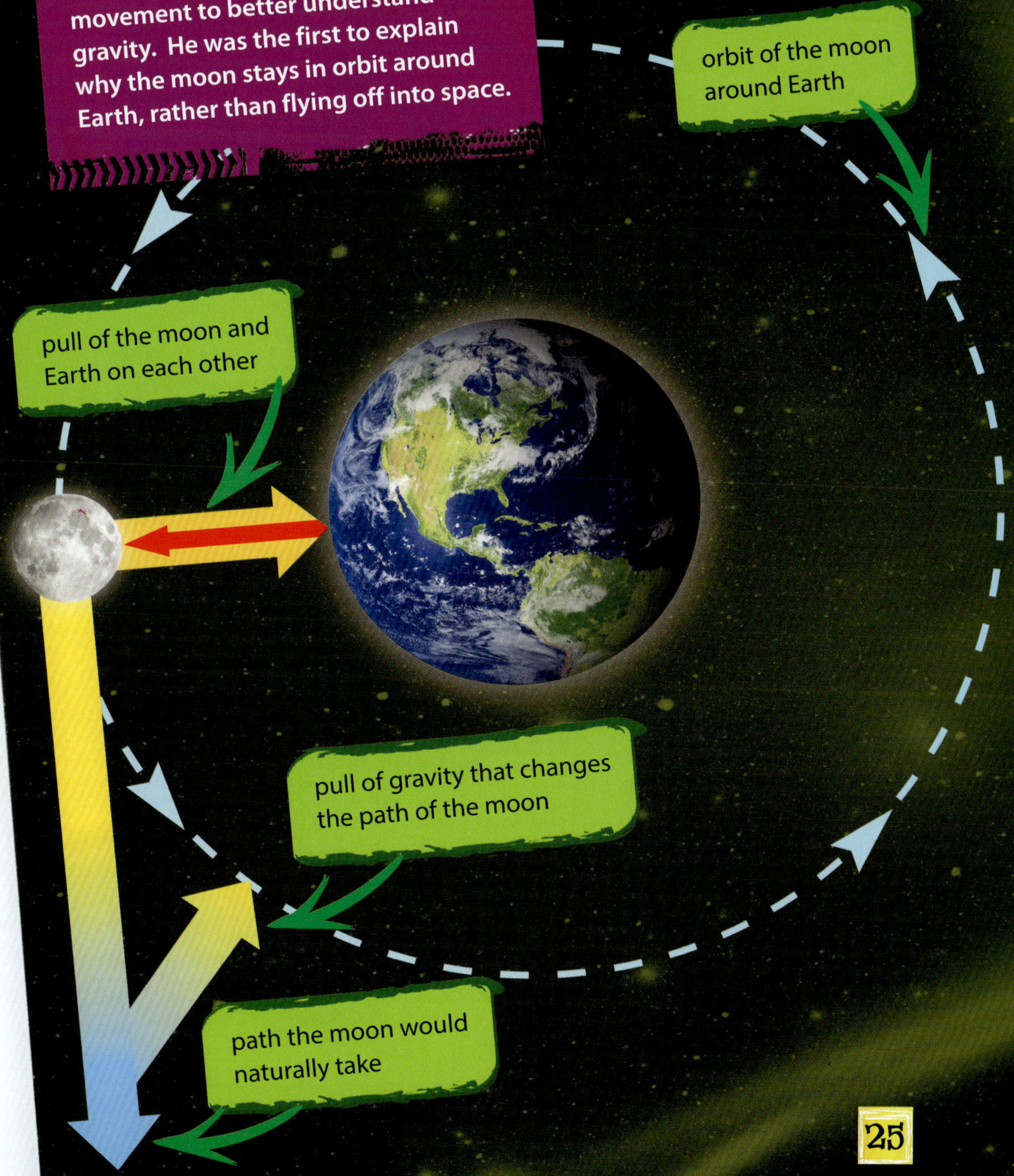

It's easy to see why people are still amazed by the moon. It's the closest **celestial** (suh-LES-chuhl) body to Earth. At times, it is only 363,105 kilometers (225,623 miles) away! And, it's the only place in space that humans have landed. So far, only 12 people have walked on the moon.

Lunar Timeline

Prehistoric Times
People observe the moon's phases. They celebrate it with myths and legends.

4th century BC
The moon's distance from Earth is measured for the first time.

15th century
The moon's motion is understood mathematically.

17th century
Scientists study the moon using a telescope for the first time.

The moon still holds many mysteries. There are more questions to ask and answer. People around the world are working to make traveling to the moon safer and easier. Someday, finding the answers to our lunar questions may be as easy as stepping out into our own backyard!

International Observe the Moon Night is held in early fall during the waxing gibbous phase.

18th century
The moon is used to navigate oceans.

19th century
Scientists try to understand how the moon's craters were formed.

20th century
Humans land on the moon. Robots and satellites are used to study the moon.

Future
Will humans one day live on the moon?

Think Like a Scientist

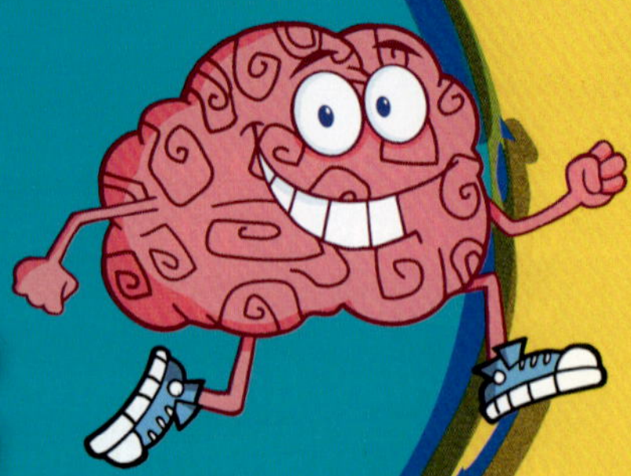

How do craters form on the moon? Experiment and find out!

What to Get

- candy sprinkles
- cocoa powder
- pie tin
- rocks of different sizes
- white flour

What to Do

1. Spread an inch of flour into a pie tin. This represents the rock that lies under the surface of the moon.

2. Sprinkle a spoonful of candy sprinkles across the flour. The sprinkles represent rocks and other material beneath the surface of the moon.

3. Shake a layer of cocoa powder on top of the sprinkles and flour. This represents the dusty and rocky surface of the moon.

4. Drop a rock into the pie tin. You can throw it at an angle or drop it straight down. Your rock represents a meteorite crashing into the surface of the moon. Repeat your experiment with different rocks at different angles. Record your notes in a log like the one shown below.

	Size of Rock	Angle of Impact	Changes in the Top (Cocoa) Layer	Changes in the Middle (Sprinkle) Layer	Draw the Impact Pattern
rock 1					
rock 2					

Glossary

astronomers—people who study stars, planets, and other objects in the sky

celestial—relating to the sky

craters—large, bowl-shaped holes in the ground made by meteorites or other celestial bodies

crescent—a curved shape that gets smaller at two points

gravity—a force that acts between objects, pulling one toward the other

lunar—relating to the moon

observed—watched and listened to something carefully

orbiting—traveling around something in a curved path

revolves—moves around something in a circular path

waning—becoming smaller

waxing—growing in size

Index

Your Turn!

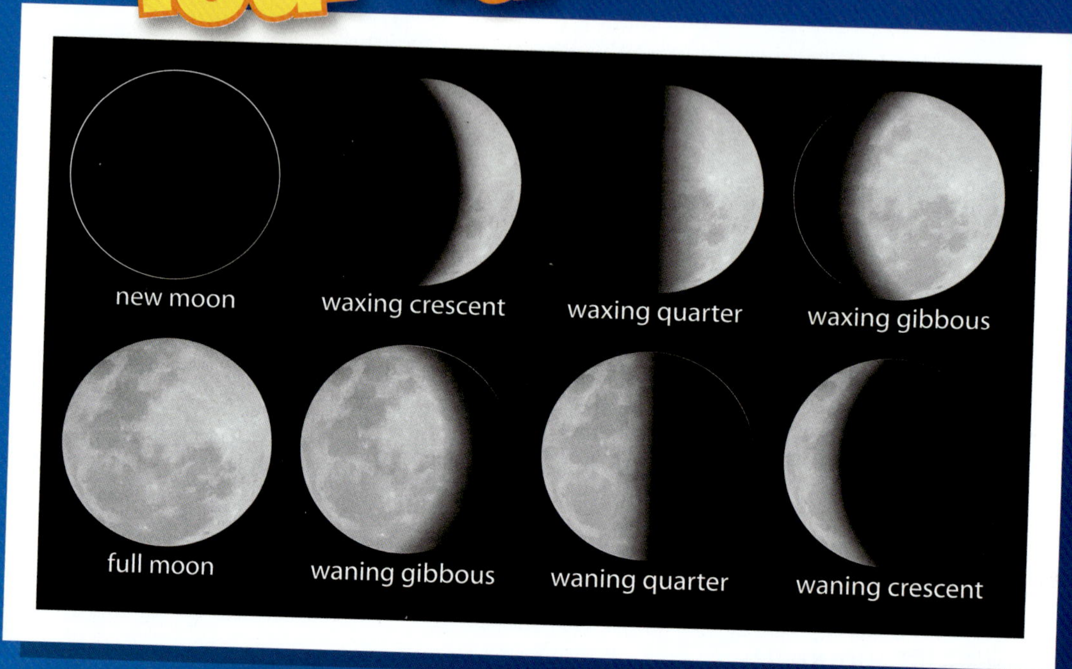

Moon Gazing

Study the chart of the moon's phases above. Then, look at the moon. Can you determine which phase the moon is in? Try to re-create the moon's phase using a flashlight and a ball. In a dark room, shine the light on the ball until it looks like the moon you see outside.